"IMPROV ABC IS A GREAT RESOURCE FOR STUDENTS
AND COACHES ALIKE. YOU CAN READ IT COVER TO COVER,
FLIP TO YOUR FAVORITE CHAPTER FOR INSPIRATION,
OR USE THE HANDY BULLET POINTS AS A CHECKLIST FOR
YOUR OWN EXPLORATION."

KATIE NUNN, IMPROV SHOP INSTRUCTOR

IMPROV ABC
BEN NOBLE

"WHETHER YOU'RE A SEASONED IMPROVISER, OR A BABY
LEARNING THE ALPHABET, THERE'S A LOT TO TAKE AWAY
FROM BEN NOBLE'S BOOK."

PEOPLE AND CHAIRS IMPROV

INTRODUCTION

When I was younger, I was incredibly impatient. Even before the days of text messages and Twitter, I couldn't stand waiting. I'd count down the weeks to summer vacation only to find myself bored just a few hours later, counting down the days until the school year started once again.

Even now, as a functioning adult (debatable), patience is a virtue I do not practice. Even if I'm enjoying a perfectly good book, I can't stop checking the Kindle progress bar with every virtual turn of the page. I am always waiting for the next thing. The next step. The next level.

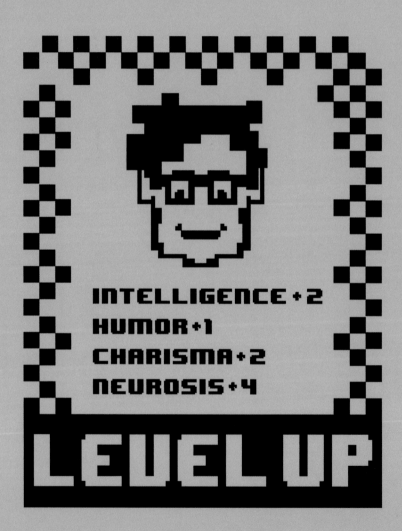

INTELLIGENCE+2
HUMOR+1
CHARISMA+2
NEUROSIS+4

LEVEL UP

The way I approach improv is no different. I listen to podcast after podcast and read interview after interview, and in each one, the subject talks about how long it takes to get good at this — five years, ten years, your whole life. It drives me nuts.

To quote Veruca Salt from Charlie and the Chocolate Factory, "I don't care how, I want it now!" And my guess, if you're reading this book, is that you want it now too.

The trouble (or blessing...depending on how you look at it) is, that unlike cooking, there is no recipe for learning how to improvise. It's all about instincts. Since every show is different, you can only study patterns and styles and learn how to apply them in theory. That way, when you're presented with a new situation, you know how to act.

The irony of writing a guidebook to improv is not lost on me. You'll hear again and again that improv doesn't have any rules. You can never prepare for an exact moment because there's no guarantee it will ever come. And while that may be true, there are better strategies and stronger choices you can make.

You can develop good habits. You can sharpen your instincts and learn to recognize patterns so that you can adapt and thrive in any show with anyone. You can learn methodologies and take advantage of tools that will make you unstoppable in any scene.

HOW TO USE THIS BOOK

In the chapters that follow, I've outlined 26 of the most important improv concepts, each beginning with a letter of the alphabet. And while you can certainly read this book straight through, each chapter stands on its own. Feel free to skip ahead, jump back, and return to the book when you need helpful reminders...or a swift kick in the butt.

And the best part is that these aren't big theoretical ideas that take hours of study or previous improv training to understand. They're simple, straightforward tips and tactics that you can apply in your show tonight. How's that for instant gratification?

A IS FOR AUDITION

Eventually, you are going to have to audition to secure stage time. And that's scary. It's the one time in improv that you're actually competing against your fellow improvisers rather than working with them.

We see auditions as zero-sum games – "if this person is chosen, then I am not." And it's true; if someone else succeeds, that's one less spot for you. The challenge, though, is not to think about them as zero-sum with winners and losers.

One of improv's key tenets is to make your scene partner look good. Despite the paradox, in an audition setting, this principle is even more important. The better you make your competitors look, the higher your odds to be chosen for that team.

WHEN TO MAKE YOURSELF LOOK GOOD	WHEN TO MAKE YOUR SCENE PARTNER LOOK GOOD
	• AUDITIONS
	• IN REHEARSAL
	• DURING A SHOW
	• IN DA CLUB, EVEN WHEN HIS DANCE MOVES ARE TERRIBLE

The best improvisers don't try to be the funniest. They don't try to bulldoze every scene with an amazing premise. They don't try to play above their scene partners. Instead, they're supportive.

They say "yes and" to other's ideas. They edit decisively. They jump on stage even if they don't have an idea for an initiation. They share the stage and let others play while they listen patiently on the sidelines. They act with kindness and generosity, both on stage and off.

Of course these improvisers are going to be chosen in their auditions. They're the people who are easy and fun to play with. The person who's trying to be funny and one-up everyone else isn't the one who looks best to the casting directors. He or she comes across as the one who's most frustrating to play alongside and the hardest to incorporate into the ensemble.

3 TIPS TO SUCCEED AT AUDITIONS

Go in with fun (not funny) as your primary objective. *This is your opportunity to play with a different crew of improvisers. It's stage time in front of a captive audience (even if they are your instructors or directors). And it's another opportunity to improvise. How could that be bad?*

Don't overthink it. *When the audition ends, you're inevitably going to mull over everything you could have done, turning an objectively good audition into a subjective disaster. Obsessing over it isn't going to change what's already happened. If you leave feeling as though you did your best, then no matter the results, consider it a success.*

Create your own opportunities. *If you aren't cast, you can feel sorry for yourself and wait for the next audition to come along or you can make your own luck. Produce your own show. Start a new team. Whatever you do, keep creating.*

"REMEMBER, YOU DON'T KNOW IF YOU ARE GOING TO BE PICKED OR NOT. THAT IS OUT OF YOUR CONTROL. WHAT YOU DO HAVE CONTROL OVER IS WHAT YOU CREATE. NOBODY BUT YOU CAN STOP YOU FROM DOING IT. THAT IS YOUR POWER."

JIMMY CARRANE, IMPROV NERD

B IS FOR BRAVERY

Most performers, from ballet dancers to the President, have the benefit of knowing what's going to happen when they take the stage – from a choreographed dance routine to a written and rehearsed speech.

Taking the stage with no script and no plan takes some real guts. It's almost silly not to feel nervous before a show, waiting in the wings for the host to introduce your team.

But improv requires more than just the bravery to show up, take the stage, and perform a scene about divorce, roommate tension, aliens, or all three.
You have to be brave enough to:

- *Enter a scene after an edit when no one else does, even if you don't have an idea for the initiation.*

- *Cut a scene, either at its highest point when it's getting a ton of laughs or at its lowest point when it's bombing.*

- *Wait for the laughs to come instead of mugging to the audience or selling out the scene.*

- *Satirize taboo subjects in a respectful yet humorous way.*

- *Show your insecurities and make yourself vulnerable.*

- *Trust that your teammates will support you.*

- *Go down with the ship.*

- *Really feel.*

Nothing happens in this life if you don't put yourself out there.

"ACCORDING TO MOST STUDIES, PEOPLE'S NUMBER ONE FEAR IS PUBLIC SPEAKING. NUMBER TWO IS DEATH. DEATH IS NUMBER TWO. DOES THAT SOUND RIGHT? THIS MEANS TO THE AVERAGE PERSON, IF YOU GO TO A FUNERAL, YOU'RE BETTER OFF IN THE CASKET THAN DOING THE EULOGY."

JERRY SEINFELD

C IS FOR CHARACTER

Character is one of those things that's easy to let fall by the wayside. It's something else to add to a mental checklist already overloaded with to-do's like having a clear initiation, realistic object work, etc. In the end, you can fall into the trap of playing it neutral in hopes that the content of the scene will carry you forward.

That said, playing neutral can be a strong choice...when you're doing it for a reason. For example, grounding the scene when your partner goes to crazy town. But playing neutral simply because you don't know what else to do (or don't want to deal with character) can hamper creativity, weaken the scene, and stall your growth as a performer.

So what are some other options?

GET INTO CHARACTER

Use the audience's suggestion. *Think of its qualities, the places it's used, how it makes you feel, and let some aspect of the suggestion inform your character. If someone says "hammer," you could be a construction worker. Or, you could think about how hammers are made of metal and choose to be a cold, no nonsense mob boss.*

Create a point of view. *Choose one thing to believe about the world. It could be that everything ties back to the bible or that animals are more important than humans. It doesn't have to come out in your first line (or at all), but having it in the back of your mind will help guide your choices and take you away from playing neutral.*

Borrow the point of view of someone you know well. *Whether it's a parent, a sibling, or your parole officer, try to choose one specific way they approach or see the world and use that as your guiding personality trait.*

Once you take a few characters for a spin, you'll find one or two that really click – either because they feel natural or because they get a lot of laughs. Use them as tools in your arsenal and bust them out when the moment's right. Just remember that they're options (like playing yourself or playing neutral), and aren't automatically the right choice. You should always explore new characters based on what the scene calls for.

PLAY YOURSELF

That should be easy, shouldn't it? You just walk on stage and react however you normally would. The only issue is that when you do that, you end up acting like you would any day – muted, polite, socially calibrated.

When my boss asks if I can stay late, I start to internally freak out and throw a little temper tantrum in my brain. But on the outside, I act totally cool and unaffected so I don't get fired. To play yourself in improv, you have to let that little man or woman in your brain come out. You can't be coy. The audience has to see how you really feel deep down. They came to the theater to see something happen, not watch two people make polite small talk.

You have to let your internal reaction guide your external reaction.

THE NUMBER ONE RULE OF CHARACTER

Above all else, when you walk into a scene and choose a character, you have to commit. Bailing does the scene a bigger disservice than coming in with no character at all. Stick to your guns and see what you can discover. At worst, you'll get a few laughs simply for playing a weirdo.

"WHEN YOU WALK INTO A SCENE AND CHOOSE A CHARACTER, YOU HAVE TO COMMIT."

D IS FOR DIRECTOR

Are you a member of a regularly practicing improv team?
Do you have a director or coach?

If not, it's the best investment you can make (even better than that $5, 24oz PBR). No matter how long you've been improvising or how good you are, it's difficult to honestly and accurately note your own shows. And it's even harder to build trust and harmony among the team if you're giving each other notes.

Newbies and veterans alike can benefit from a director's impartial eye. They can help you and your team shore up weaknesses and explain concepts in a new way that may make more sense. They also have their own opinions about improv and their own style, which can help you grow in different ways.

There's nothing wrong with forming a "for fun" practice group and jamming together, but if you're serious about improvising, the fastest way to get better is under the supervision of a coach you respect and trust.

Don't feel the need to be overly loyal to one director. Everyone brings their own point of view and perspective to a team. Change your coach up every six months to a year to keep things fresh and to make sure your team keeps exploring and growing.

ON THE FLIP SIDE

Are you a director or coach? Are you an aspiring director or coach?

New improv teams are forming every week. Ask around and see if anyone's looking. If you've completed a series of classes and perform regularly, you're probably ready.

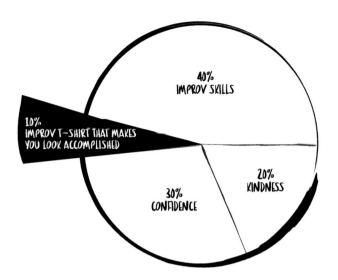

40% IMPROV SKILLS

10% IMPROV T-SHIRT THAT MAKES YOU LOOK ACCOMPLISHED

20% KINDNESS

30% CONFIDENCE

Coaching is one of the best ways to give back to the community while simultaneously growing as an improviser. You will be asked difficult questions. You'll design lessons plans. You'll identify and focus on players' strengths and weaknesses. You'll be responsible for providing feedback, both positive and negative, in a constructive, kind way. You will be the team's greatest supporter.

COACHING TIPS

Believe in yourself. If you're a coach, you're being paid for your expertise. There is no "right way" to do improv. You can only share your own experience and perspective. Don't be afraid to answer questions, lead exercises, or give feedback. There are no objective truths.

Admit when you don't know something. If you aren't sure how to answer a question, say you're not sure. Ask other improvisers you know and respect. Take some time to think about it. Then, answer at the next session.

Steal from your coaches. Most of them have been in the game longer than you have, studied at other training centers, and coached before. Repurpose their exercises and alter them to suit your team's needs.

Experiment. Like improv, your coaching should go with the flow and follow the fun. Create exercises that hone in on the team's objectives. Try new forms. Change the lesson plan if you're not feeling it. Do wacky stuff that might not have any direct effect on the team's form or style.

Listen. You're the team's employee. Help them work on what interests them.

E IS FOR EMOTION

Improvisers are actors – actors with superpowers, because they don't have the benefit of costumes, scripts, props, lights, sounds, or weeks of rehearsals. But They are still actors, which means it's their responsibility to play believable, emotional scenes.

No one came to the theater to watch you play neutral. If that's what the audience wanted to see, they could just go to a restaurant and watch a new couple try to play it cool on a first date.

Fortunately, anyone can act. You can play any believable emotion – happy, sad, frustrated, despondent, lustful – because, at one point, you've all experienced those feelings. The challenge is that once you finally figure out what's going on in the scene and how you feel about it, a lot of times, the scene is already over.

"HOW DO YOU GET OUT OF YOUR HEAD? FEEL."

JOE BILL, CO-FOUNDER OF ANNOYANCE THEATER

To access those rich emotions, we have to play scenes that force us to react immediately.

Don't wait to have an opinion. *If the first line is something provocative and emotionally charged, react however you normally would. If it's something neutral, make a choice about how you feel and let that define your character. You'll be faking it at first, but as the scene continues, you'll start to actually feel it.*

Use your body. *When we're sad, we fold our arms. When we're confident, we puff out our chests. But this also works in reverse. It's been proven that how we carry our body affects our mood just as much as our mood affects our body language. When you want to play a specific emotion, put your body into it, and mentally, you'll start to feel it.*

Discover what you want vis-à-vis the other person. *It's one thing to want to move to New York. It's another thing to want to move to New York to audition on Broadway even though your mother (who is also your scene partner) wants you to inherit the family farm. The first scene will only scratch the surface. The second example will be a deeper scene that touches on real, relatable issues.*

Waiting to make a choice and feeling out the scene hampers your ability to play emotionally. Taking a risk and quickly determining how you feel (and then discovering why) gets to the meat faster, helping you access real emotions.

The best scenes I've done are the ones where I feel what I'm playing; when I'm real mad, not just "acting mad." Then it's not even acting. It's something better. It's something real.

F IS FOR FORM

When a new improv team is born, one of the first questions that comes up is what kind of form they should play. Obviously size, style, and personal preferences play a role in the decision, but more often than not, the debate over form is an exercise that should come much later in a team's lifecycle.

F could just as easily stand for "forget your form." Like the photographer who is more concerned about the quality of his camera than how to properly set up a shot, the improviser who prioritizes form over content is bound to fail.

When I was first starting out, I played on a duo-improv team called Minstrel Blood. Since there were only two of us, we decided to perform monoscenes, but we weren't content to leave well enough alone. Before we felt comfortable with the complexities of the monoscene, we decided to add a layer of difficulty by performing SCRAM, an intricate monoscene-esque form pioneered by two improv greats, Jill Bernard and Joe Bill.

Perhaps it was an ill omen that we ignored, but Minstrel Blood debuted SCRAM at 7:30 AM on a Saturday morning as the final set of a 12 hour, all-night improv festival to an audience of seven other comedians in a near zombie state. When we decided to scrap the fancy form and get back to basics a few shows later, our scene work dramatically improved.

WHY YOU NEED FORM

Form allows you to share a common language with your fellow improvisers. The type you choose controls how your team explores themes and makes broader statements about the world through comedy. But a good form is like good design or good writing – it's best when it doesn't draw too much attention to itself. When the audience is spending time thinking about the form, that's time they're not spending watching what they actually came to see – good improv.

When it comes to choosing a form, the best advice is to put it off as long as possible. Focus on your scene work. Build a strong foundation. Then debate form to your heart's content.

"A GOOD FORM IS LIKE GOOD DESIGN OR GOOD WRITING — IT'S BEST WHEN IT DOESN'T DRAW TOO MUCH ATTENTION TO ITSELF."

G IS FOR GAME

Humans love patterns. Recognizing them is one of our greatest triumphs as a species. That ability separates us from the savages, like black bears, wolves, and your mother-in-law. For some reason, patterns also make us laugh.

Think about your favorite sketch. Odds are, once you strip away the details, the thing that makes it funny is nothing more than a simple, repeatable pattern. Take SNL's Debbie Downer – someone makes a positive statement, Debbie recontexualizes it negatively. We laugh. Repeat. Repeat. Commercial break.

That's all game is – a simple pattern to guide the scene forward and make the audience laugh. And the best one's are, as Debbie Downer proves, incredibly obvious.

"FOR ME GAME OF THE SCENE IS A METAPHOR: GAMES HAVE RULES, AND SO CAN SCENES. IT'S UP TO THE PLAYERS TO FIGURE OUT THOSE RULES AS THE SCENE DEVELOPS. THE RULES CAN BE WAYS IN WHICH THE CHARACTERS BEHAVE OR REACT, PATTERNS TO THE WAY THEY THINK, OR RULES GOVERNING THE SITUATION OR EVEN THE WORLD IN WHICH THE SCENE EXISTS."

KEVIN MULLANEY, ARTISTIC DIRECTOR AT UNDER THE GUN THEATER

I: RELATIONSHIP AS GAME

A lot of improvisers know that the relationship – who the two characters are to one another – is key to moving a scene forward. Equally important, however, is discovering how those characters behave in that given relationship.

If the scene is between a son and father, is the son rebellious and the father authoritarian? Or, are they best buds that get into trouble together? Any choice is fine, the key is to recognize the pattern and stick with it. Following and heightening that relationship will keep the scene focused and funny.

II: GAME AS GAME

While all scenes need a relationship, there are plenty of times when it takes a backseat to premise. For example, you and your scene partner might play a scene about two mechanics that one-up each other about how they've ripped off customers. The game isn't about how the mechanics feel about each other; rather, it's about how they interact with the world around them. They can just heighten how they've ripped off customers until the scene ends.

III: GAME AS SPICE

Some "game as game" games (wow...this sentence) aren't strong enough to carry the scene on their own, so they get demoted to "game as spice" games. For example, imagine a premise where two knights speak to each other using modern slang. The idea is funny, but it's subtle. As soon as the two knights start talking about how they're not using period-accurate language, the joke crumbles. This type of game must be paired with one of the other two games types above. But when done right, this game can add another layer of humor to what's already in progress.

RELATIONSHIP AS GAME

- REBELLIOUS SON AND STRICT FATHER.

- TWO GIRAFFES WHO DREAM OF FREEDOM.

- A COUPLE TRYING TO HAVE A BABY.

GAME AS GAME

- MECHANICS BRAINSTORMING NEW WAYS TO RIP OFF CUSTOMERS.

- BUSINESS OWNERS PITCH WACKY IDEAS FOR A NEW VENTURE.

- A PRESIDENT WHO MAKES INCREASINGLY DICTATORIAL CHOICES.

GAME AS SPICE

- COWBOYS WHO USE SMARTPHONES.

- KNIGHTS WHO USE MODERN SLANG.

- A YOUNG GIRL WHO CALLS HER PARENTS BY THEIR FIRST NAME.

H IS FOR HONESTY

A lot of outsiders mistakenly believe that to succeed in improv, you must be quick-witted or funny. We let outsiders believe that because it makes us feel smarter than we really are. The best comedy, however, comes from sharing personal experience through vulnerability and honesty, which is way simpler than being witty or funny.

But just because you have the source material – your life experience – doesn't mean it's easy to use. It can feel awkward revealing your deepest insecurities to a packed house full of strangers. There are a few things, though, that can make the process easier.

WEAR YOUR CHARACTER LIKE A THIN VEIL

The father of long form improv, Del Close, recommends wearing your character like a thin veil, which, in English, means that you can play anything from an army general to a stay-at-home mom, so long as you let a bit of yourself shine through. Give that general your same fear of disappointing your parents. Give that mom your high school experience. See what that does to make your characters more raw and more real.

Don't worry about letting the audience in on your love for smelling sweaty socks or your creepy obsession with Flower from Bambi. Since you're acting, they'll assume it's all made up.

KNOW THAT EVERYONE IS A WEIRDO

Each one of us feels that we are the only person in the room who is afraid of the dark or worried that we'll never find Mr. Right, but our deepest and weirdest insecurities are often (nearly) universal.

When you bring them up, know that the audience isn't laughing at you. Quite the opposite. They're laughing out of recognition. They see your vulnerabilities in themselves, and it makes them feel like they're not alone in the world. Comedy isn't just about making people laugh. Comedy also has the power to comfort and heal.

"COMEDY HAS THE POWER TO COMFORT AND HEAL."

I IS FOR INSPIRATION

As with most new improvisers, when I first started, I said "yes" to any and all improv-related opportunities. Before I knew it, I was attending two or three shows a week, practicing with three different independent teams, taking classes, and generally abandoning any commitment that didn't involve my new improv friends.

THINGS TO DO:

- ☑ HANG OUT WITH IMPROV FRIENDS
- ☐ CALL MOM
- ☐ EAT
- ☐ SLEEP
- ☐ SEE OTHER FRIENDS
- ☐ WORK OUT
- ☐ MASSAGE MY CAT

Most new improvisers follow that same path. I'm not sure if that's a product of improv communities – which are super welcoming and fun – or if it's just the type of person who signs up for improv – obsessive, friendly, and incapable of saying no.

While the conventional wisdom is that spending more time (like 10,000 hours) practicing something will make you a master, with improv it's best to let your mind recharge to stay inspired and avoid burnout. Earn those 10,000 hours slowly.

Your scene work is only as good as the personal experiences you bring to the table, and you can only have those personal experiences when you spend time away from improv and enjoy everything life has to offer.

8 COOL NON-IMPROV THINGS TO DO THAT WILL GET YOUR CREATIVITY FLOWING

· Go get coffee with someone you don't know very well
· Go on a walk and leave your phone at home
· Travel
· Try a new artistic medium or teach yourself a new skill
· Teach someone something
· Call an old friend and catch up
· Read a book or watch a movie on a subject you don't know much about
· Go see live music or (non-improv) comedy

9 COOL NON-IMPROV BOOKS THAT WILL GET YOUR CREATIVITY FLOWING

Steal Like An Artist and **Show Your Work** *by Austin Kleon*
Contagious: Why Things Catch On *by Jonah Berger*
The Accidental Creative: How To Be Brilliant at a Moment's Notice *by Todd Henry*
On Writing: A Memoir to the Craft *by Steven King*
Made To Stick: Why Some Ideas Survive and Others Die *by Chip Heath*
Freakonomics: A Rogue Economist Explores the Hidden Side of Everything
by Steven Levitt and Stephen Dubner
The Tipping Point: How Little Things Can Make a Big Difference
by Malcolm Gladwell
One More Thing: Stories and Other Stories *by BJ Novack*

In the beginning, it's good to throw yourself fully into improv. You get the reps in and start to see immediate progress and improvement. But as you advance, there's no faster way to improve your play than to be intentional about the commitments you take on. That way, you have plenty of time to seek inspiration in the things you love, which makes your performances even better.

Once you take a little time off or reduce your commitments, it's amazing how improv won't seem like "work" anymore. You'll feel more creative and scenes will flow much easier.

J IS FOR JUDGEMENT

When given the opportunity, people are quick to point out their shortcomings and slow to list things they do well. After improv shows, it happens all the time. You and your teammates huddle in the back room and your coach asks how you think the show went. Most of the comments sound like this:

"Our edits could have been tighter."
"I shouldn't have done so many walk-ons."
"Our group games were weak."

And rarely do you hear things like:

"Our first beat scene had a clear, strong game."
"Your tag out killed."

Just like one negative Tweet can make us forget the 100 supportive ones, the moments in which we fail shine so much brighter than those in which we succeed.

In improv, as with most things in life worth practicing, you're never going to be as good as you want to be. There will always be someone better to look up to – either in your own community or on SNL actually getting paid.

Ironically, that's a good thing. It's a great motivator to keep improving. If you felt like you were awesome at improv, you wouldn't be challenged and you wouldn't feel the need to keep growing. You'd be bored.

One of the first things you must accept is that you're never going to have the perfect show – improv is an art form that's entirely made up on the spot. There are always going to be things to work on.

Don't walk off stage feeling sorry for yourself because it wasn't an A+ event. Feel good knowing you did something most people would pee their pants trying once. And remember, the audience often thinks the show went much better than you do.

Before you start listing everything that went wrong, take a few moments to celebrate the things that went well. You've got your whole life to keep improving, but you only have a few minutes to stand back and marvel at what you created.

ON JUDGING OTHERS

Don't. It's a waste of time and energy and it goes against the very spirit of improv.

Much has been written about "that guy" (see Will Hines Improv Nonsense Blog) the improviser that seems to crop up in every jam or class, who you feel is not technically skilled, has poor comedic taste, or makes "bad moves."

There is nothing you can do to "fix" this person, and the sooner you realize you can use your own skills to "yes and" them and just play, the better off you'll be.

They may not be a skilled improviser or perhaps you just disagree on what makes for "good improv." Either way, the only person you can affect on stage is you. It's unproductive to spend time judging them or complaining. At least they're putting themselves out there and having fun. They're trying to grow as a performer.

By standing on the sidelines with your arms crossed in disgust or by "suffering" through a scene with them, you're the one not "yes and-ing." You're the one not supporting your scene partner. You're the one who is the problem, not them.

CIRCLE THE ONE
WITH A PROBLEM

K IS FOR KILLJOY

If you're reading this book, it's because you want to be better at improv. But the weird thing is that the more you want to be better at improv, the more likely it is that you won't be.

When you're busy worrying about making "the right moves," you sacrifice the ability to play spontaneously, have fun, and live in the moment. When you're in your head, you're not having fun, and when you're not having fun, how is your scene partner supposed to have fun? And if neither of you are having fun, how is the audience supposed to have fun?

Improv is a team sport. The best shows are those where the responsibility and moves are equally shared among all players, but that world is a fantasy world much like Westeros, Middle Earth, or the land of Classical Economics. We all feel as though we bear more of the burden to "carry the show" than everyone else.

A year ago, one of my students was struggling with trust. She trusted her own skills but felt the need to "save the show," even when the show didn't need saving.

To those of us who have felt that way, our intentions are noble. We want the team to have the best show possible. We want everyone to succeed. But at its core, this feeling is cocky and disrespectful. The underlying assumption is that we're better than the rest of the team and they need us to make them look good.

Now you kind of feel like a jerk, right?

Obsessing over making "the right move" and constantly trying to save the show kills the joy – yours and your teammates'.

"I THINK THAT IF YOU ARE TRYING TO PLAY FROM A PLACE OF TRYING TO PROVE SOMETHING TO THE AUDIENCE OR TRYING TO PROVE SOMETHING TO YOURSELF OR TRYING TO MAKE 'IMPROV MOVES,' YOU'RE NOT REACTING OR LISTENING, YOU'RE JUST PLANNING EVERYTHING AHEAD OF TIME OR TRYING TO DO SOME SORT OF THING INSTEAD OF NATURALLY REACTING TO THE THING THAT'S HAPPENING AROUND YOU. SO IT'S NOT VERY COMPELLING TO WATCH. IT FEELS HOKEY."

ALEX HONNET, FOUNDER OF THE UPSTAIRS GALLERY

The success or failure of any show does not rest on your shoulders alone (for better or for worse). You don't need to steer the ship. If you're on a team, you have to trust that your teammates are just as smart and funny as you are. So don't worry about making "the right move," because there is only one "right move" – follow the fun. Find joy in creation.

L IS FOR LAUGHTER

For an improviser, laughter is both a blessing and a curse.

There's no better feeling than walking on stage and getting a chuckle from your initiation or first response. It bolsters your confidence and can help you identify the funny part of the scene – game or relationship – that you should focus on.

On the flip side, there's no worse feeling than thinking "this line is going to kill" only to be greeted by crickets, cell phone taps, and ice clinking in glasses. It's during these moments where our mettle is tested. Do we stay the course or do we panic and sell out?

NEVER BAIL

Bailing on the scene is never the answer, no matter how painful pushing forward might feel. It's always better to go down with the ship than to sell out for a laugh. "Sell out" moves include...

- Calling "cut" as if you're the director of a film that's gone horribly awry.
- Denying or saying no to your scene partner to make them look crazy.
- Breaking the fourth wall and providing commentary on the scene.
- Getting X-rated out of nowhere just to provoke an audience reaction.

Yes, it's honorable to stay the course while the scene collapses around you, and it's also the stronger improv move. Any kind of gimmick in which you mug to the audience for a laugh constitutes a denial of everything you've built together – even if what you've built totally sucks.

Every one of the above tricks will, in all likelihood, provoke an audience reaction, but the laughs aren't worth it. You let fear win. You end up denying your scene partner and sacrificing him or her to save yourself, and there's no more selfish move than that.

Rather than bailing, the best thing you can do is to take a deep breath, tell the fear to shut up, and be patient. Look at your scene partner, take a moment to assess where you are, and reinvest in the scene you already have.

- Discover something deeper about the relationship.
- Make a confession.
- Pick up something in your environment and see where object work leads.

Get back to the fundamentals of scene work – "yes and," listening, honesty, and vulnerability. You will probably get your scene back on track and find the funny.

YOU DON'T HAVE TO MAKE THEM LAUGH

When most people hear "improv," they immediately think "comedy". But just because audiences are attending shows expecting to laugh, that doesn't mean it's your responsibility to make them.

All improv does not have to be comedic. The art form can be used to play a range of human emotions and explore topics that can be serious, dark, or cathartic. Making the audience laugh is satisfying. Captivating them, discovering a deeper truth about our shared human experience, and forging a real connection can be even more powerful.

M IS FOR MONOLOGUE

Monologues are one of my favorite ways to open a show because each one is personal and unique. The way someone sees the world, the little things they remember, and the lessons they've learned reveal themes and details that lead to scenes we don't see every day.

THE DIFFERENCE BETWEEN THEME AND DETAILS

With all of the information you hear during a monologue, how do you know what to use for your initiation? The answer lies in sifting everything into two categories: themes and details.

Details are the small things that tickle you, like a specific name, the type of clothing someone wore, the specific song that was on the radio, etc. Themes are bigger. They're the lessons or morals that the monologist learned, like never trust your older brother, don't talk to strangers, and listen to what your mother tells you (or maybe that last one's just me).

Scenes are stronger when you initiate with a theme as your pull. They lead to universally understood premises ripe for exploration. Initiating with details like, "hey, that's a pretty floral dress," will get a laugh (because the audience will make the connection), but you're not giving your partner much to work with. Starting with something like "Mom, I should have listened when you said not to ride my bike at night," will be much more fruitful.

That isn't to say details are unimportant; they're best used as seasoning to an already awesome, theme-based scene.

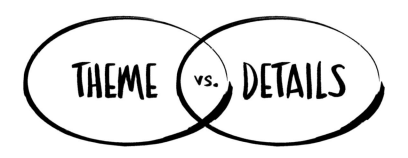

HOW TO DELIVER THE PERFECT MONOLOGUE

Delivering the perfect monologue is easy. It only requires you follow the same basic principles that make for a great scene.

Step away from the suggestion. If the audience says pineapple, you don't have to talk about how much you love pineapple. You can step as far away as you'd like so long as you show the audience your thought process by saying, "pineapple makes me think of Hawaii, which makes me think of vacationing, which makes me think of when my family went to Alaska." Then tell that story.

Follow the last thing said. You may not know where the monologue is going when you start, but you can't go wrong as long as you keep asking yourself "why?" and "so what?" You may end up somewhere totally different than you intended, but the audience will be engaged as you move from fishing with your dad to the last time you went to the aquarium, so long as you logically follow the last thing said.

Be honest. Explain how you felt and why. Give every detail you can remember. This will give your teammates plenty of ammo to play with. And don't talk about how you "always used to do something." That won't be as rich as the one specific time a thing happened.

Don't try to be funny. Your honest commentary on the human experience will connect with the audience and make them laugh more than jokes.

You don't need a button. As you're delivering your monologue, think about the moral or the point and drive toward it. But if it's unclear, let your teammates figure it out through scene work. Never end with something like "and that's my pineapple story." It cheapens the monologue and is unnecessary. Monologues don't need to come to a clear conclusion (just like scenes are often cut in the middle of conflict). End on a laugh and return to it later.

"SCENES ARE
WHEN YOU
WITH A
AS YOUR

STRONGER

INITIATE

THEME

PULL."

N IS FOR NOTES

Teams both welcome and dread the post-show notes. They serve as a reminder that some things went well and other things went...not so well.

If the show was awesome, the notes may inspire us to improve. If we bombed, the notes are an annoying reminder of our mistakes. But if we didn't want to get better, what would be the point of performing?

IF YOU'RE RECEIVING NOTES

Find the note within the note. *You're never going to do the same show twice, which means that a note on a scene may not ever apply again. Try to find the deeper meaning of the note (Disagreement? Lack of environment? A weak character choice?) and apply it more broadly.*

Take them with a grain of salt. *At their core, notes are your coach's opinion. You always have the right to disagree with or disregard a note. However, take it into consideration and give their advice a try before moving past it.*

Only focus on one or two things at a time. *Depending on how often you practice and perform, you could receive several notes in a single week or month. And while we want to fix all of our weaknesses at once, our brains can really only focus on one or two concepts at a time. Make progress on what you find most important, then give that concept a break and work on something else.*

IF YOU'RE GIVING NOTES

Give your overall opinion first. Your players generally know how the show went before you open your mouth. If it was good, start by congratulating them and indicate that the notes are improvements on what was already great. If they bombed, they know they bombed, so don't dwell on specifics and belabor each mistake. They probably just want to grab a drink and forget the whole thing.

Be direct. If improvisers have completed training and play regularly, they are passionate about improv and want to get better. They want you to tell them what's good, what's bad, and how to fix it. It's a waste of everyone's time to tiptoe around negative feedback.

Don't single people out. In contrast to being direct, it's best to give notes in the "we" form, like "we could have had a clearer game in 2A." In improv, we succeed or fail as a team. Our notes should be a reflection of that collective responsibility.

"THE JOB IS NOT TO SUCCEED BUT FAIL MORE INTERESTING THAN THE LAST TIME — IN A MORE SUBTLE FASHION OR IN A MORE INTRIGUING WAY."

TJ JAGODOWSKI, MISSION THEATER

O IS FOR OBJECT WORK

When first starting out, most of the improviser's mental energy is expended on creating engaging and funny dialogue, which makes object work seem like an unnecessary distraction. But worrying about the conversational content leads to "talking heads" scenes, in which the players simply have a conversation sitting or standing around without much action.

Improv is a visual medium. The audience has come to see us play. Otherwise, they could have just listened to the radio.

Talking head scenes should be avoided because they're boring to watch and they hamper the improviser's ability to live in the moment. When we're not grounded in the physical, we can only talk about what we make up rather than discovering something through the environment. Standing around burdens us with the freedom to overthink, plan, and invent things, which makes for lamer scenes.

"IMPROV IS A VISUAL MEDIUM. THE AUDIENCE HAS COME TO SEE US PLAY."

WHAT CAN YOU DISCOVER THROUGH OBJECT WORK?

Your environment. *Walking around the space or picking things up helps the audience see what you're seeing, whether it's a kitchen or a playground. The environment also defines how the characters might behave. For example, a scene between a boss and her employee would play out differently in the boss' office, an elevator, or a park.*

Your mood. *In a talking heads scene, mood can only be conveyed via dialogue and physical reaction. Object work, however, can underscore your choice. Do you sweep the floor in a slow, melancholy way or do you do it quickly and in secret? It can also help you determine your scene partner's intentions if you watch how they interact with objects before initiating.*

Truths about the scene. *When improvisers feel stuck in scenes, one trick is to make a confession. Another helpful trick involves picking something up from your environment and talking about what it means. If two roommates are discussing their messy apartment, you can prove it true by picking up a two week old pizza box and see where to go from there.*

REMEMBER...

As an improviser, you have control over your environment. If you are the Dan Quale of object work, you have the option to make it easy on yourself. If you can't operate an espresso machine and do the scene, why not start by holding a full mug of Joe?

Don't talk about what you're doing. When you rake leaves with your dad, you talk about sports or your deadbeat brother, not his lawn care technique.

P IS FOR PATIENCE

As a millennial, I hear a lot about my generation's obsession with instant gratification. I can talk to anyone, anywhere in the world, in seconds. I can order a product from Amazon, and it shows up a few days later. Now. Now. Now.

Everything they say about me is true.

From the first day I started taking improv classes, I wanted to be the best. There's nothing wrong with that. A lot of improvisers feel the same way. That desire moves us forward. It pushes us to complete classes, join teams, and get back on stage even after we bomb.

But the impulse to be the best can also be a great source of frustration. It sucks when you're not getting good fast enough. There's an impulse to give up as soon as you feel that you've plateaued.

Mastery of improv – or any creative pursuit – requires practice and time. The first you can control. The second involves ancient black magic that I cannot go into detail about here.

PRACTICE + TIME = MASTERY

Improv newbies tend to follow a similar path – they jump in headfirst. They take classes, form independent teams, perform as soon as they're allowed, and go to every show they possibly can at the expense of food and sleep. This constant practice develops and hones the core skills, and it helps them do it faster than someone who only does improv during class. But practice can only help someone grow so fast.

"KNOW THAT IT'S A REALLY GOOD THING THAT IT'LL TAKE A WHILE TO GET HALFWAY DECENT AT IT. THAT YOU CAN'T RUSH IT. AND DON'T TRY TO RUSH IT. YOU'LL COME ALONG AT THE PACE YOU'RE SUPPOSED TO COME ALONG AT. DON'T THINK OF IT AS MATH. IT'S MUSIC. IT'S NOT A PROBLEM TO BE SOLVED. IT'S A SONG TO BE LISTENED TO."

TJ JAGODOWSKI, MISSION THEATER

You cannot control time. You have to let it pass at its typical, languid pace while you absorb everything you can along the way. You need time to see more shows and steal from your favorite performers. You need time to play on different teams with different people with different skill levels. You need time to work with coaches and directors who approach the art form in new ways.

The desire to be really good, right here and right now, hinders your ability to live in the moment and be fully present. It can make your continued study of improv seem silly and futile at times. Or maybe, it makes it that much more important.

Q IS FOR QUESTIONS

On the first day of improv – aside from learning where to find the bathroom, who the cute boys or girls are, and how weird your teacher can be – you learn not to ask questions in your scene work.

In a perfect world, every line uttered, every object interacted with, every facial tick, sigh, and body weight shift should add information that moves the scene forward.

Questions simply don't do that. They spawn from a deep, dark place of fear, shifting the burden of creation onto your scene partner. They force him or her to come up with new information rather than just supplying it yourself.

As Tina Fey elegantly puts it, the flipside of "don't ask questions" is "make statements." Newer or more timid improvisers don't do this because they are afraid they'll say the wrong thing.

The fearful improviser will say, "How are you feeling today, Amy?" instead of looking at their scene partner – the way they're standing, how they're interacting with the environment, their facial expression – and saying, "You look so sad, Amy."

"THE TRUTH IS THAT ANYTHING YOU SAY IS THE RIGHT THING, BECAUSE IN IMPROV, THERE ARE NO WRONG ANSWERS."

BUT I HAVE BEEN LYING TO YOU

Just like your third grade math teacher who said you couldn't take the square root of a negative number, the rule against asking questions isn't steadfast. It's a training wheel that you can take off with practice.

Questions are fine so long as they add information that moves the scene forward.

In the above example, if the improviser had said, "You look sad, Amy. Is it because you got kicked out of the Justin Beiber concert?" she would have added new information – that her scene partner had been kicked out of a concert. From that single question, we can begin to make assumptions about their location, their age, their personalities, what the scene is about, etc. And based on the rule of "yes and," the scene partner should take the gift of this new information, say yes, and build on it.

Next time you want to ask a question on stage, ask yourself this first – why am I asking a question? If it's because you need help understanding what's going on in the scene, make a statement instead. If it's what your character would do, then go for it.

R IS FOR RELATIONSHIP

Improv is about people interacting on stage. Nothing else.

Unlike other mediums, there are no props, sets, costumes, or scripts that allow you to translate your vision to the audience. All they can see from their seats are two people, two chairs, and a stage, so focus on those things. Start by figuring out who those two people are and what they mean to one another.

"STOP TALKING ABOUT RELATIONSHIP. IT'S A MOOT POINT. OF COURSE IF THERE ARE TWO CHARACTERS IN A SCENE THERE'S A RELATIONSHIP. IT'S LIKE SAYING HUMANS BREATHE AIR. CHARACTERS HAVE RELATIONSHIPS. BUT THAT'S NOT THE FUNNY PART. THE FACT THAT YOU'RE MY DAD ISN'T FUNNY. IT'S THE UNUSUAL ASPECTS OF THIS PARTICULAR VERSION OF THAT TRADITIONAL PAIRING THAT WE FOCUS ON."

CHRIS GETHARD, THE CHRIS GETHARD SHOW

The relationship you and your scene partner establish at the top (ideally within the first few lines) provides the filter for everything else going forward. Anything that happens from that moment on has to somehow relate back to the relationship, so it's important to start off with something strong, clear, and fun. Hopefully it will be something different and unique too.

KEYS TO A KILLER RELATIONSHIP

Define it. Spend as little time as possible trying to figure out who you are to one another. Not defining the relationship is the quickest way to tank a scene. Period. Because, if nothing else, you can always go back to that connection if you're feeling stuck.

Address each other like real people. When I talk to my brother, I don't walk over to him and say, "Hey bro." I say, "Hey Jordan." There are so many ways to show the audience he's my brother without saying it, from physical closeness to speaking with familiarity to talking about our mom.

Decide what's different today. Most real relationships are static, which is boring to watch. In improv, it's your job to discover the conflict. Make today the day where you confess something big or finally bring up that issue that's been bothering you. Or do the total opposite by playing something as close to real life as you can, complete with all of its intricacies. But make sure it's about something. This doesn't mean there has to be an argument or a fight. It just means the scene needs to be about something and your characters need to be affected by it.

Don't talk about someone or something else. The audience didn't come to the theater to watch you talk about someone or something they can't see. Figure out how that external force (like the child who isn't in the room or your grandma's antique trunk) impacts the relationship between the people on stage.

Same goes for specifics. Improvisers are taught to use specifics to establish the relationship. However, don't just make up a story about being a troublemaker in third grade if it has no bearing on the present. If you tell that story, your character is either still a troublemaker or the scene is about how you've grown out of causing trouble. Everything from the past must affect the present.

Grow. People grow. Relationships change. Be affected by the information you discover and be open to change, especially in longer scenes.

S IS FOR SUGGESTION

At the top of their infamous improv show, TJ Jagodowski and David Pasquesi walk on stage, tell the audience to "trust us, this is all made up," go to blackout, and then start their set.

In the world of long form improv, the idea of not taking a suggestion seems heretical. After all, doesn't the suggestion lay the groundwork for the entire show?

Yes. But no.

When we go to the audience for a suggestion, we get a lot of the same, unhelpful stuff like bathroom or pineapple. But how often do we use those suggestions to actually inform the entire show? In most long forms, there is some sort of opener used to tease out more information, or players might jump into a tangentially related scene and use that as a basis for inspiration. Other times, the suggestion gets ignored completely.

"NOTHING DRIVES ME MORE NUTS THAN WHEN PLAYERS GET A SUGGESTION OF 'CHEESE' AND IN ABOUT FOUR SECONDS THEY GO FROM BRILLIANT TO STUPID AS THEY TRY TO MENTION THE WORD CHEESE OVER AND OVER AGAIN IN EVERY SINGLE SCENE. WE GET IT: THE SUGGESTION WAS 'CHEESE'."

JIMMY CARRANE, IMPROV NERD

Experienced improvisers use the suggestion as a springboard to discover something deeper about the relationship between the two characters. It's rarely the focus of the entire scene, and even if it were, chances are the work would suffer.

In the end, the suggestion serves as nothing more than the contract between the players and the audience that this really is all made up.

WHAT TO DO WITH A SUGGESTION

For the sake of this section, let's pretend we're given a suggestion of violin.

Use it to inform your environment. People play violins in a concert hall, or the band room in a high school, or at a metro station. You could start a scene in any of these places and initiate with whatever you want to talk about – like about how you're the worst player in the symphony or that you have a crush on the band teacher or even something about your ex-wife.

Use it to inform your character. Violins are delicate, beautiful, and precious. They're also difficult to understand. You could create a character around any of those adjectives – someone sensitive, someone obtuse – then, you can initiate with whatever you want to talk about.

Ignore the suggestion. If nothing's coming to you or you're getting tripped up, just let it go. Choose the character you want to play. Initiate something that seems interesting. You'll find that the suggestion has a funny way of magically showing up in the scene anyway.

The suggestion is exactly that – a suggestion. It's not a roadmap. It's not a rulebook. It's just something to get your juices flowing and help you start creating something out of nothing. Treat it as such.

T IS FOR **TEAM**

Improv is a team sport. While other creative pursuits like playing an instrument or dancing include an ensemble, in these instances, the necessary skills can be practiced alone and each individual has a chance to stand out.

In longform improv, there are no solos and there isn't an easy way to practice by yourself. The best way to improve is to form a team as early as possible, in your first level or two of training. Ask around and find likeminded classmates who are interested in forming a practice group and get to it.

Don't be afraid to ask people who you think are "too busy" or "too good." You never know who might be interested in improvising with you.

THINGS TO DO ONCE YOU HAVE A TEAM

- Start practicing regularly.
- Choose a time and place each week and meet there.
- Hold each other accountable and use practice time to actually practice.
- Find a coach and pay them to teach you.
- Hang out, get to know each other, build trust, and share common experiences (outside of practice time).

ARE YOU READY TO PERFORM?

Yes. You are.

Getting in front on an audience as quickly as possible is the best way to get better. It's the time when all of your training comes together and is tested, revealing the team's strengths and weaknesses moving forward.

Don't wait until you graduate training or until you "feel ready." That'd be like practicing soccer for a year without actually competing against another team. No matter how hard you train, that first exhibition isn't going to go super smoothly. The more shows you do, the less messy they'll get.

HOW MANY TEAMS IS TOO MANY?

Newer improvisers have an admirable tendency to dive in headfirst and join many teams. More experienced improvisers focus on one or two. The answer to "how many is too many" comes in the form of another question – how much can you handle without getting burnt out? It's a balancing act that only you can answer.

PROS
- Improvising with many different people helps expose you to new things and helps you grow.
- You'll get more stage time and more opportunities to practice.
- Different coaches can help you understand concepts in a new way.

CONS
- You may burn out.
- If all you're doing is improv, you won't have time for any other experiences that will help inform your scene work.

A NOTE ON VERSATILITY

When you see shows, be on the lookout for improvisers you admire. These could be people who have a style you'd like to develop or players who make moves you'd never think up in a million years. These are the people you should be asking to join your team.

While it's fun to perform with your best friends and classmates, it's more important to build a team full of players that complement your strengths and weaknesses and can help you grow through practice. The more you play with those kinds of improvisers, the better you'll be at augmenting your own strengths with the kind of moves they'd make, which helps you become a more well-rounded player.

U IS FOR UNIFORM

Improv is a pretty casual performance art. There aren't any costumes. There isn't a lot of practice before each show. There isn't a lot of hubbub on the day of. Since you just show up and make stuff up, you generally just show up in whatever you're wearing that day too.

Some theaters have a dress code. For example, performers at The Second City must wear dress shirts, ties, nice pants, and blouses (sometimes all at once). But independent teams performing in bars across the world can wear anything they want.

I like to be comfortable as much as the next guy. I wear jeans and a t-shirt or button up to the office every day. So I get that no one wants to dress up more than they have to.

There are all those overused career platitudes like "dress for success" or "dress for the job you want, not the job you have," but those are sayings for a reason. People take us seriously when we step up our fashion game. If your lawyer walked into the courtroom wearing an Avengers t-shirt and flip-flops, you'd probably plead guilty and get it over with.

In any show you perform, the odds are high that at least one person in the audience has never seen improv before, so they'll take the art form as seriously as you do. You can have the best show of your life, but if you perform it in a tank top, the audience may not appreciate it as much.

Dress for every show like it's a first date – a nice top (a polo, button down, blouse, or nice sweater), good pants (casual khakis, nice jeans). For those new people in the audience, this is a first date... just with improv instead of someone sexy. We need to make a good impression to land that second (and third, and fourth) date with our troupe.

"EVEN IF YOU DO IMPROV STRICTLY FOR FUN, YOU'RE PUTTING ON A SHOW FOR AN AUDIENCE. HOW YOU PRESENT YOURSELVES IS AN OPPORTUNITY TO STAND OUT FROM THE DOZENS (MAYBE HUNDREDS?) OF OTHER TEAMS IN THE CITY... BOTTOM LINE? LOOK LIKE YOU'RE WORTH PAYING TO SEE PERFORM."

PEOPLE & CHAIRS IMPROV

V IS FOR VOICE

When you're first starting out in a new artistic medium, you suck. You suck because you haven't had enough practice. You suck because you haven't taken enough lessons. You suck because you haven't seen enough finished product to understand the good from the bad.

So you steal. You start watching other people. You start defining your taste. You practice, suck, keep practicing, and eventually, you get better. And through repetition of this process, you begin to establish yourself and define your unique voice.

You define your voice by the types of scenes you like to play, the kinds of characters you enjoy, and the forms you love. But the best improvisers are those who, rather than having a single, distinct voice, play with many.

"THE ONE THING THAT YOU DON'T FIGURE OUT AS AN IMPROVISER OR A SKETCH PERFORMER IS 'WHAT AM I?'"

JORDAN PEELE, KEY AND PEELE

Every show is different. You never know what tonight's set will call for — a slow, patient scene about a dying wife with cancer or a fast, gamey scene about two frat boys one-upping each other. Maybe the show will need you to edit. Maybe it will need you to do a killer walk-on.

Unlike other art forms where the goal is to differentiate yourself and stand out, in improv, the goal is to blend in. You should always try to support your teammates and the show, no matter what it calls for. Even if that means abandoning your awesome idea or your normal style of play.

The phrase "jack of all trades, master of none" might come to mind. It serves as a cautionary tale, encouraging artists to specialize in one discipline rather than try to do everything. In improv, however, mastery of one aspect is less important than proficiency in all things.

The best way to stand out and define yourself in improv, ironically, is by having the ability to let go of your ego, walk on stage, and give the piece exactly what it needs, every time.

W IS FOR
WHO/WHAT/WHERE

Early on in classes, you learn that the perfect initiation covers the who, the what, and the where of a scene. As you grow as an improviser, those types of initiations can start to feel heavy-handed and unnatural.

Consider this initiation – "Hey sis, glad I found you in the kitchen. I want to tell you I'm gay."

No one talks like that. If improv is intended to reflect life, then opening with a stilted, unnatural line is not a good way to start.

More importantly, an initiation that establishes the three W's doesn't leave any room to build something with your scene partner. If you take a little more time and use the first five to ten lines to discover the who, what, and where, you'll not only sound more natural, but you'll be working together and truly improvising.

Remember, not all of the information needs to be conveyed through speech. You can use all the tools at your disposal, such as, object work, physicality, and side play to communicate your intentions to the audience and to each other.

In our example, object work, like washing a plate, could be used to establish the kitchen location. A male player could pull another male teammate from the sidelines to be the boyfriend. When walking on, the brother could hug the sister to indicate emotional closeness. And then he could point to the boyfriend and initiate with a line like, "Karen, I have something very important to tell you. Please don't tell mom and dad."

Now, doesn't that sound much better?

"WORK ON THE WHO, THE WHO, AND THE WHO. ADD SOME WHO, AND THEN EXPLORE THE WHO. THE WHAT AND WHERE WILL REVEAL ITSELF."

TJ JAGODOWSKI MISSION THEATER

COUNTERPOINT

Some forms are less organic than others and involve openers or build on previously established source material. In contrast to the previous section, if you've got a great idea for a scene and you're using material from somewhere else, establish the three W's up front. That way, there's no confusion between you and your scene partner about what you're trying to set up.

In organic or premise based scene work, clarity trumps realism.

AN EXERCISE TO TRY

The Ten Line Scene

You and a partner play a scene sharing ten lines between the two of you. A line, in this case, means a sentence, so "Hey Steve. You look good today. I really like that shirt," counts as three. Once you've used all ten lines, stop and consider what could have been cut to get to the heart of the scene faster.

X IS FOR X-RATED

We've all watched a comidian or listened to a podcast where the speaker keeps dropping the f-bomb over and over and over. The first time you hear it, you're like "f**k yeah!" The second time, you let it pass by. The fifth time, you just want them to stop saying it. And by the seventh, you never listen to their show again.

I've certainly been known to use my share of four-letter words or make the occasional sex joke to churn up some laughs, but in almost all instances, getting X-rated in your set is unnecessary.

When four letter words become filler, equivalent to "like" or "um," you're doing it wrong. They rarely add much to the scene, and in the end, reflect poorly on you.

KEEP IMPROV PG-13

Getting X-rated is lazy. The English language is made up of 1,025,109 unique words. It's lazy to reach for the most provocative just to get a reaction. Same goes for crude scene work. There are tactful, funnier, and more meaningful ways to cover the same ground.

Use words sparingly to preserve their power. There's a time to break out the f-bomb or the c-bomb, and that's when your character simply has no other choice. If those words are part of your regular repertoire, however, they won't come across with the same force when you do need them.

Think about your audience. Most people come to your show knowing it isn't appropriate for their 10-year-old nephew, but occasionally your teammate's whole family show up with a kid in tow. Imagine if they never saw another show simply because you couldn't get through a scene without using a four letter word or making a sex joke. Keeping it PG-13 seems like the easiest way to avoid turning people off to improv.

"I WOULDN'T SAY THAT WE WORK HARDER, BUT WE HAVE TO BE MORE WELL-ROUNDED THAN SOMEBODY WHO CAN RELY ON AN EXPLETIVE TO GET A LAUGH."

DIANAH DULANY, COMEDYSPORTZ HOUSTON

Y IS FOR YES AND

"Yes and" seems to be the one rule everyone and their grandma knows about improv. It's the one concept that's invaded corporate culture and creative circles because it's simple and useful. You accept what's presented to you, and then you make it even better.

After their first class, students know that if their scene partner says, "our daughter bought you this tie," you never say, "But we don't have a daughter." It brings the scene to a screeching halt because there is no agreement on the reality of the scene.

So when your scene partner says something, you accept it and then you find a way to add to it, moving the scene forward.

Don't say "no." Simple.

But simple does not always mean easy. In real, live improv, things can get hairy. We can fool ourselves into thinking we're yes and-ing even when we're actually denying our scene partners.

WHERE THE EQUATION BREAKS DOWN

Problem 1:

One note I find myself giving students is that they need to "and" harder. They believe that saying yes, then adding affirmation is enough, but all that does is accomplish the "yes" part, leaving your scene partner to come up with even more information.

Player 1: Wow, this car is so roomy.
Player 2: Yeah! There's so much space in here.

In this example, all Player 2 has done is restate Player 1's idea that the car is big. They haven't actually created anything new, like a killer stereo system or the expensive price tag.

MAKE EVERY STATEMENT COUNT. EVERY CONTRIBUTION SHOULD MOVE THE SCENE FORWARD, NOT JUST CONFIRM THAT WHAT YOUR PARTNER SAYS IS TRUE.

Problem 2:

As improvisers improve, they also get better at finding clever and unique ways of denying their scene partners. So good, in fact, that they don't even realize they're doing it.

Example
Player 1: (excitedly) I've gotten everything packed for the cruise!
Player 2: You know I hate cruises. I'm not even excited.

While the example reads like a scene we've watched before – a scene that may have even been funny, entertaining, and enjoyable – Player 2's response is not a true yes and. It feels like one because they agree to the reality, that two people are about to go on a cruise, however, this is an example of yes but. "Yes we are going on a cruise, but I hate cruises so let's fight about it."

Instead, Player 2 should have said something like, "wow, you really know how to take care of your wife!" That way, Player 2 still says yes to the idea of the cruise but moves the scene forward instead of getting hung up on why Player 2 planned a vacation knowing Player 1 would hate it.

That isn't to say the "I hate cruises" line is wrong, but It creates an artificial conflict that probably isn't as rich as one we could discover if we focus on adding information and exploring the characters rather than the situation.

Yes and is the simplest and most powerful move in the improvisers tool belt. The better you get at truly yes and-ing, the more opportunities you have to create memorable scenes.

Z IS FOR ZOINKS

ZOINKS
Exclamation. Usually from surprise or delight.
Shaggy: "Zoinks Scoob, we are out of Scooby Snacks"
–Urban Dictionary

For an art form that allegedly has no rules, there are a lot of things to think about when the lights come up and you find yourself on stage. We've filled every letter from A to Z with something you ought to keep in mind. But the secret is just that – all of these "rules" are nothing more than things to keep in mind.

After I had studied improv for two years, my Harold team coach, Katie Nunn, said she was going to write all of the rules of improv on a whiteboard. This is all she wrote:

"DON'T EVER F***ING BAIL"

That's it.

That one phrase covers all of the rules explored here, from A to Z. You don't f***ing bail on your scene partner because you yes and them. You don't f***ing bail on your teammates because you're brave enough to initiate or edit, even when you don't have a good idea. You don't f***ing bail on yourself because you take credit for what you do well and don't judge yourself or your teammates when weak moves are made.

The best improv happens when you internalize all of the rules and just enjoy the moment. It's one of the hardest things to do because we all have that killjoy inside of us who is screaming that we aren't good enough and don't know the right move.

In reality, the only right move, the most important rule, is to never stop taking risks and trying to surprise yourself. Never be afraid to pull out a crazy character, try a weird accent, or cut a scene that needs it. Never be afraid to create something and commit.

"I WAS A CLASSIC BIG-PICTURE PLAYER WELL ONTO MY THIRD HAROLD TEAM AND THEN SOMETHING HAPPENED. MY TEAM WAS HAVING SOME SORT OF FUN THAT I FELT LIKE I WAS MISSING OUT ON. I REALIZED EVERY OTHER PLAYER ON THAT TEAM WAS TOTALLY IN THE MOMENT, AND I WAS STILL THINKING ABOUT THE PIECE. DON'T EVER FORGET THE NUMBER ONE SKILL WE HAVE TO KEEP DRILLING OVER AND OVER IN OUR CAREERS IS WALKING INTO THAT TWO-PERSON SCENE AND BEING TOTALLY PRESENT IN THE MOMENT."

KATIE NUNN, THE IMPROV SHOP

No two nights are ever the same. If we wanted to do a show over and over to perfection, we'd have done scripted work. The joy of improv is the joy of not knowing what's going to happen when the lights come up. It's the joy of creating something in the moment with a supportive group of friends.

If you accept that the only improv rule is to never f***ing bail, then know that the best way to get better isn't to memorize everything in this book. In fact, you could throw this book out the window right now.

Tonight, you're going to get on stage, you're going to forget everything you just learned, and you're going to have one, simple goal – give the audience, your teammates, and even yourself no choice but to shout "zoinks!"

ACKNOWLEDGEMENTS

This book would not have been possible without the help of the following people:

Julia Madras – for believing in the idea from day one, supporting me throughout the process, and being an exceptional Mr. Manager.

Jodi and Mike Noble – for pushing me to be my best, giving good feedback, and always being "very proud."

Steven Harowitz, Katie Nunn and Jake Eshelmen – for generously giving their time to read my first draft and provide invaluable feedback.

Miles James – for his sharp design thinking and support.

Chryssi Yip and Stephanie Phillips - for their editing savvy.

The members of the Nefarious Bakers and 30 Rock From The Sun – for honing my coaching skills, taking my advice, and making me look and feel like a rock star.

THANK YOU!

ABOUT THE AUTHOR

Ben Noble is a writer and improviser in St. Louis, MO. He's the founder of I'm Making All This Up, an organization dedicated to helping creative dreamers bring their ideas to life. He performs regularly at St. Louis' Improv Shop as well as in his bi-monthly improv show series around the city. He teaches improv workshops to corporate groups, beginners, and intermediate performers looking to level up. He also has a cat, so that's neat.

To learn more about Ben, or to hire him for an improv performance, workshop, or speaking engagement, visit immakingallthisup.com or email him at *ben.noble91@gmail.com.* He promises to write back and he'll even include a fun GIF.

Made in the USA
Monee, IL
08 October 2021